See Me Through My ABCs

By:
Dr. Rachel H. Francis, RPh.

Illustrated by:
Hatice Bayramoglu

Published by Melanin Origins LLC

PO Box 122123; Arlington, TX 76012

Copyright 2022

First Edition

Library of Congress Control Number: 2022903046

ISBN: 978-1-62676-378-4 hardback

ISBN: 978-1-62676-439-2 paperback

ISBN: 978-1-62676-438-5 ebook

This book is for "Resilient Reese", my son. I pray you always keep your happy spirit and your loving eyes. When you can't find the words to say... let me be your voice and advocate. And when you speak – may you be heard by all.

This picture book is also for the parents of special needs children. May you always grant yourself grace. Each day may not be easy, but our children are worth it! Keep striving to give our children the absolute best.

Dr. Francis

A is for **acceptance**. Accept that every child is different and that is okay. At heart, *all* children want to do is play.

Reese

B is for believing. Believe a child can do anything
no matter what. Teaching is key, and no giving up.

DAILY ROUTINE

6:AM Wake up

6:30AM Breakfast

7:AM Brush teeth/get dressed

8-4 pm: Therapy center

5:pm shower

6:pm eat dinner

7:pm tv time

8:pm bedtime stories

C is for consistency. A schedule is needed for a child to succeed. Start small and stay the course, then you will see.

D is for different. I was born to stand out. I love being me. I will change the world. Don't you agree?

E is for early intervention. Resources can be your best friend once a proper diagnosis is made. Help is out there, along with services, and people at your aid.

Autistic Spectrum Conditions

High functioning autism, Asperger's or PDD				Classic Autism	
Extreme ability in some areas	Above average I.Q.	Average I.Q.	Mild learning disability	Moderate learning disability	Severe learning disability

F is for finding. The spectrum is so vast. Find what your child is great at, foster it, and it will last.

G is for **gifted.** "Differently-Abled" can mean many of things. Brilliance is one of them; take notice of talent and abilities.

H is for happy. A child's happiness is key to any success. When this happens, a child can do their absolute best.

I is for **imagery.** Vision boards or pictures help our children to learn through the day. Visual aids and planning boards help to guide them along the way.

J is for joint attention. Pointing to an object or following a gaze may be hard to do at first. Conquering this skill is best when one-on-one therapy is reinforced.

K is for **kid.** Have patience with your kid who is growing.
Development is only one part of their story.

L is for **learning**. Learning to interact and play with others is necessary for school. Being able to follow the leader and listen to commands are key jewels.

M is for **music therapy.** Music is known to help a child to learn. When you desensitize a child to sounds, the anxiety of going places will be of no concern.

N is for **nurture.** What you nurture and cultivate will grow, it's true. A child needs a lot of loving, understanding, and patience. See it through.

O is for occupational therapy. Fine, motor skills may be slightly delayed, but a therapist can teach kids to eat, walk, and play.

P is for **probiotic.** Add a probiotic to your child's diet because we are what we eat. It will help with digestion and combat brain fog; it will defeat.

Equine Theraphy for Autism

Q is for **questions.** They may seem never-ending. There are no questions too big or too small when helping your child succeed. Research, asking for help, and listening are key.

R is for **reading.** Read all that you can when you can to me. I promise I'm listening; keep at it, you'll see.

S is for **speech therapy**. A little help is needed from a speech therapist. They are trained and will help your child to articulate at their best.

T is for timeline. Try not to measure your child against another. They are all unique and can learn from each other.

U is for **understanding.** With wisdom comes understanding and our children need more of it. Try to see the world through their eyes; it surely will benefit.

V is for **victory.** Every milestone, big or small, is a victory. A child enjoys praise to continue to progress satisfactorily.

W is for **words.** Words may not come easy for kids like me, but please keep talking because I'm listening to EVERYTHING.

X is for **xerox**. A child on the spectrum is not a carbon copy of another. Each child has their own quirks and abilities waiting to be fostered.

Y is for **yearn.** Yearning for what could be or never be is something to consider. Always be thankful for it all; your child is amazing. Always remember

Z is fo **zigzag.** As you zigzag your way through your child's life, remember to have fun. Ups and downs, twists and turns, before you know it...it's done.

About The Author

Dr. Rachel H. Francis is a licensed pharmacist in Louisiana and Texas. She devotes her time to patients, providing them with the care they need and deserve. While **Dr. Francis** isn't working or fulfilling her passion of writing and volunteering, she is a wife and mother to two exceptionally made children. Her life is her family and she wouldn't have it any other way.

Dr. Rachel Francis is a believer and she thanks God for all of His many blessings, lessons, and opportunities. Stay tuned for more inspirational literature.

CPSIA information can be obtained
at www.ICGtesting.com
Printed in the USA
BVHW011419290322
632742BV00009B/133

9 781626 764392